W9-BZW-955

The Precious Moments Of Mothers

The Precious Moments Of Mothers

by Angela Grace

Illustrated by Samuel J. Butcher

BALLANTINE BOOKS
NEW YORK

A Ballantine Book
Published by The Random House Ballantine Publishing Group
© 2003 Precious Moments, Inc.
Licensee: The Random House Ballantine Publishing Group,
a division of Random House, Inc. All rights reserved.

All rights reserved under International and Pan-American
Copyright Conventions. Published in the United States by
The Random House Ballantine Publishing Group, a division
of Random House, Inc., New York, and simultaneously
in Canada by Random House of Canada Limited, Toronto.

Ballantine and colophon are registered
trademarks of Random House, Inc.

www.ballantinebooks.com

Library of Congress Cataloging-in-Publication Data
is available from the publisher upon request.

ISBN 0-345-46208-4

Book design by Julie Schroeder

Manufactured in the United States of America

First Edition: May 2003

1 3 5 7 9 10 8 6 4 2

*O*ur lives are
made up of Precious Moments.

She is the most important person in your life.

She brought you into this world,
cared for you, and helped you to become the
wonderful person you are now.

She is your mother.

She also set the standard for you to follow
as a mother yourself.

How to raise children, care for them, teach them,
and prepare them for their lives.

So many memories.

So many Precious Moments.

These are the Precious Moments of Mothers.

$\mathcal{D}$o you remember . . .

... when you were just a little girl?

You'd say your prayers each night.
"Now I lay me down to sleep,
I pray the Lord my soul to keep.
If I should die before I wake,
I pray the Lord my soul to take."
Your mother and father taught you that prayer,
    as they had taught you many others.
They were good parents, and you knew that one day it
    would be your turn to be the teacher.
One day you would be a mother yourself.

...all those silly stories you heard when you were little?

The type of stories that answer questions like "Where do babies come from?"

None of your friends really knew...so they made it up.

The baby store, the stork—no one knew, and no one would admit it.

But your mother knew.

She told you that babies came from heaven.

When you asked for more details (like how they came down from heaven), she just laughed, and perhaps answered with the usual, "Maybe when you're older."

You said, "Okay"...and wondered to yourself, maybe the stork really is part of it?

*...when you were
still a little girl and
you used to play "Mommy"?*

Sometimes you used your dolls, other times a carriage
full of puppies (who sometimes played along and
other times made for the most mischievous of
baby surrogates).

You played this game very seriously.

You wanted to get it right.

Most important you wanted to treat your babies
right.

Just like your mother...

...and just like the mother you hoped to be one day.

Playing the game was fun, ill-behaved puppies and all.

But you knew it was just a game.

For now.

6

. . . when you learned to care?

You were still very young and had not yet turned an
eye toward boys or even remotely considered a
future family of your own.
You just realized one day that it felt good to care
for another living thing, to feel its life and its
affection, and to try to give it a better existence.
Petting a cat's fur caused it to purr, and snuggling
with a bunny caused it to nuzzle.
You discovered that caring was its own reward.

. . . your mother's first lesson to you?

She said, "Follow your heart."

She wasn't talking about boyfriends and romance (though they would play a part later on). She was talking about that little light that resides in all of us, that sense of right and wrong, and that instinct to reach out and love.

All of the answers lie within.

Maybe not the details of the where and when or the how much and how far, but the real answers—the right and the wrong.

She taught you that the answers lie within.

. . . when you looked in the mirror and saw your mother's eyes?

They were always so peaceful and full of love like the
   calmest pool on a beautiful spring day.
Even when you were both upset, you could count on
   the peace that dwelled within her eyes.
It was the peace of love, a mother's love shared
   with you.
Then one day you looked in the mirror and there
   they were.
You had grown up and you had your mother's eyes.
And they were filled with love.

*...when you realized
how similar little children
are to sheep?*

They are so soft and innocent and ready to follow.
Like a good shepherd, it's the mother's job to protect
her flock from harm, to keep them warm and
provided for until the day they are ready to set
themselves apart from the flock and make it
on their own.
Maybe that's why little children are often compared
to precious lambs.

... when you first looked at the world through a mother's eyes?

Your bundle of joy had not yet arrived, and certain
   details of the world around you began to stand out.
Cats with kittens.
Dogs with puppies.
Even birds nesting.
What a perfect thing nature is! Mothers care for their
   young—no instruction necessary!
Unfortunately not everything comes naturally to us.
That's why there are plenty of books to read and
   classes to take.
But love is a mother's instinct, linking us with the rest
   of nature in a great circle of motherhood.

... when you baked your first pie?

Your mother had given you the recipe, the one that
    your grandmother had given to her.
It was the first time you had made it on your own,
    and you were so proud.
This was your pie, and there would never again be
    anything like it.
Your mother smiled.
She, too, was proud.
You were her daughter, and she had taught you well.
And she knew that one day you, too, would be
    looking proudly at your own daughter as she
    beamed with pride over her first pie.
Mothers make the best teachers.

...the first home
you could call your own?

It was just a little place, large enough for "two plus"
   who had plenty to give and a love to share.
It was the place for your growing family.
When you moved in it was just a house, but with your
   "two plus" it became a home.

...when you were expecting?

Sometimes the time dragged, while other times the
   days flew by.
There was so much to do, so many preparations,
   blankets, bottles, and other baby things to buy.
Everything had to be just right.
It had to be perfect, and you had to be ready for that
   wonderful day that was quickly approaching.
And you would be.
Love was the blanket that would keep you warm and
   ward off the fears about things to come...and it
   would also be there to warm your little bundle of
   joy on the day it arrived.

... when all of the insignificant cares fell by the wayside?

Sure, you had some ups and downs.

You couldn't sleep, your stomach felt queasy, and
you felt awkward and bloated.

To say that you felt uncomfortable was an under-
statement.

And then one day you looked in the mirror
and realized that none of those things really
mattered.

You had a baby inside of you who was ready and
restless and waiting to come out.

It was a little human life, and you were its mother.

And nothing else mattered.

...when you first felt
the little one inside of you,
what a beautiful thing it was?

A seed had become a sprout that had grown into a
    bud and was well on its way to becoming the most
    beautiful flower of them all.
It was your child!
Nature and life surround us everyday of our lives,
    all evidence of God's love for us.
His gifts to us are many, and none greater than life.

. . . those moments
right before you gave birth?

The expectation and the joy mixed with fear and
apprehension.

It was happening so fast and yet so slow.

You couldn't wait to be through with this part of the
ordeal, and on to the wonderful moment when you
held your little bundle of joy in your arms for the
very first time.

Images and dreams flashed through your mind as
you waited for the final moments.

There were no storks on hand, only angels, and
they had been entrusted with this precious human
being that was about to become a very important
part of your life.

...the first time you held the little bundle of joy in your arms?

It was a life!

You were a mother!

It was an awesome responsibility, and you knew that a lot would be demanded of you.

You prayed for strength during your difficult times.

But right then, when you held the little bundle of joy for the first time, apprehension and fear disappeared, and all you could feel was love.

...the early-morning feedings?

Getting out of bed while it was still dark and cold outside and warming the milk and bottles like your
mother and grandmother before you.

Maybe the stove was now a microwave set to an
automatic timer, and maybe the house wasn't as
drafty and cold as it had been in years gone by...
but some things never change.

Babies still need to be fed.

And mothers still love them.

*. . . when the
two of you would
rock together?*

The days were so filled with activities—you were both
    so new to all of this.
It was a welcome respite for mother and child to just
    sit back and rock the world away for a while.
Your precious would sleep in your arms, while you,
    still awake, would rest with your dreams.

. . . laying her down in her cradle?

It was that special time of day—time for her nap.

Both of you were tired, and a couple of restful hours were just what the doctor ordered.

You bundled her up in her sleeper and put her down ever so gently, nestled between blanket and pillows.

She took a nap, and you watched her sleep, until soon you took a small, much-deserved nap yourself.

...how peacefully your child slept,
a hint of a smile at private dreams
and the waiting wonders
of the world far outside
this peaceful crib?

You really wished that you could have a peek at those
sleepy-time thoughts and perhaps share them.

You wished that you could share everything with
this little bundle of joy…but knew that was not
to be.

Those private dreams were just beginning.

Soon there would be other private things.

Your bundle of joy would be on her own way too
swiftly.

And that would be okay because you would still be
there, ready to lend a hand, advice, or just an
encouraging word whenever that day arrived.

...those days
leading up to Christmas
during your first year
as a mother?

There was so much to do.

Decorations to put up, gifts to buy, meals to prepare,
all in addition to the diapers and the feedings and
the comforting of your newborn bundle of joy.

You sometimes wondered how there would be enough
hours in a day…and most of the time there was.

You might remember always being tired, but that
was a more-than-fair trade-off for the greatest
Christmas gift of all, the spark of love and
excitement in your little one's eyes on
Christmas morning.

...her first Christmas?

The days of hustle and bustle were over.

The tree had been trimmed, the gifts were all wrapped, and Christmas morning had finally arrived.

Her eyes were so wide trying to take in all of the colors and lights, the sights and the sounds of the most wonderful day of the year.

Her smile and delight filled your heart with love... and you said thank you to God for the greatest gift of all.

...holding your little one in your arms?

He was so tiny and so delicate, and when he slept he
seemed so peaceful.

You felt his rhythmic breathing and the beating of his
little heart, and occasionally he would let out a
little noise just to let you know he was there.

He was so small and you loved him so much.

He was a gift from above, and you would never let
anything take him from you.

And as he slept you said a little prayer of thanks.

...when your love
was her entire world?

She looked to you for everything.

How to act, what to say, what to do.

What you didn't tell her, you showed her by your own
example.

You were her entire world, but you knew that one day
she would outgrow its limits and dare to explore
the world on her own...and that was okay
because your love made that possible.

...when you received
your first Mother's Day gift?

Your husband always made sure that the little ones
had something to give you on Mother's Day...but
this one was special because it was given without
his help.

You later learned that it was part of a class project.
Everyone had been given seeds to plant in milk
cartons. The students cared for the plants and
watched them grow and blossom over the spring
months. Then, on the Friday before Mother's Day,
the now blooming flowers were transferred to
flowerpots for presentation to you on Sunday.

It was the perfect gift.

. . . your baby's first pet?

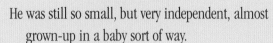

He was still so small, but very independent, almost
grown-up in a baby sort of way.

You and his daddy decided it was time to widen the
family circle.

Not another child, just yet.

Something smaller, a little pet.

His daddy brought it home one day, and together
you watched your little one's eyes go wide
with joy.

They got along fine and were soon the best of
friends.

...your first family portrait?

Your son was still so little he had to be carried in
　　your arms.

You and his daddy got all dressed up for your first
　　family portrait.

Years later when you showed this picture to him,
　　he had a hard time believing that he was ever so
　　small (and you did, too, now that he was so
　　grown-up, even though you still remember
　　that day as if it were only yesterday).

You don't need a photo to recall some memories...but
　　the pictures are nice to have anyway.

... baby's first birthday?

The year had gone by so fast, you thought to yourself,
   and my how he has grown!
Everybody agreed what a good boy he was, how smart,
   and so sweet.
Your little boy was growing up, and everybody was
   there for the celebration, with the promise of
   many more to come.
It was definitely a special day for him.
For you too.
It was the anniversary of one of the most important
   days of your life.
And you were grateful.

...how much
he enjoyed his bath?

He had so much fun, splashing around in the
   bubbles.
Sometimes he was your little sailor and other times he
   was the captain of his own soapsuds ship.
Bath time was fun time.
Just you and he together.

...those moments
of wonder and discovery?

He was into everything, more than curious, hungry
   for answers to questions unspoken.
A more precocious toddler there had probably never
   been.
"Why is the sky blue?"
"Why is the snow cold?"
"Where do ducks and chickens come from?"
So many questions, so many answers.
"Where are the birds flying to?"
"Why do they have to go away?"
"Will they be coming back?"
Sometimes he stumped even you, but that was all
   right. You could learn new things along with
   your inquisitive boy.

...his first step?

It was all very exciting, the fine art of putting one foot
in front of the other.

First he crawled, then he stood.

A wobble here, a stagger there.

He was so proud, and maybe a little frightened
(as you were, too).

But he made that step on his own and you were there,
hand extended, ready to break his fall.

That step was followed by another, and another,
and in no time you were walking together,
hand in hand, step by step.

...the joy
of watching her play?

She would mother her dolls just as you did when you
were her age.

You took special delight in watching her imitate you,
as you had imitated your own mother, and you
found yourself imagining the day when she would
be a mother in her own right.

But that was a long way off, so you just enjoyed
watching her pretend.

...his first day at school?

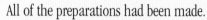

All of the preparations had been made.

Pencils sharpened, notebooks purchased, book bag
  packed, lunch made.

He looked so grown-up and ready to face the world.

Yet he was afraid to go.

But you knew he had to.

School was going to be fun, you assured him.

So he went…and it was fun.

Now he leaves eagerly for school each morning, as
  you kiss him good-bye, cherishing each special
  moment.

. . . when a mother's attention was the best first aid?

A mother's job comprises many trades, with
"emergency nurse" being close to the top of
the list.

A scraped knee, a bruised elbow, or a cut on the finger
were all easily treated with a mother's kiss, a
mother's care, and a whole lot of a mother's love.

Two lips to the bruise made the pain go away and the
tears disappear faster than an ambulance could
ever arrive on the scene…and all without you
ever attending nursing school.

...the joy of sharing treats?

Sometimes it would be the result of insistent pleas or tearful requests.

Other times it would just be a surprise.

And other times there would be no reason beyond your desire to prepare something that you knew they would enjoy.

The reward was sometimes in the process itself—the sweet smells, the yummy taste, the joy of creating—and other times in the sense of accomplishment for a job well done.

But the looks on their faces when they realized that you'd made it for them was the best part of all.

...the joy of spending time together?

Maybe it was a family vacation, going out to a restaurant, playing games, or just reading together.

As Mom, you were primarily responsible for planning and implementing even the simplest family activities.

But you didn't mind. In fact, you'd have it no other way.

Part of the fun was in seeing new places, or hearing a great story.

But most of the fun was in just being together.

...your part in the Parents' Night talent show?

You had never done anything like this before.

Getting up onstage, singing a song, and playing a musical instrument.

None of this was in the baby books and parenting guides that you had studied.

Surely this wasn't a requirement of being a parent?

But indeed, all of the other parents were doing their part, and if they were ready to strut their stuff onstage, why shouldn't you...especially since your little one was expecting you to?

So you said yes.

Who would have guessed you'd have so much fun?

*...when you first
noticed that she was
no longer just a baby, and
she was now your little girl?*

Her hair had grown out and sleeper sets and blankets
had given way to nightgowns and dresses.

And her hair began to look just a little bit like yours
when you were her age.

She even had your smile and your laugh.

She was a little person with a personality all her own,
even though she was still your baby, and you could
still hold her in your arms.

She was growing up already, but thankfully not too
fast.

...when that sense of loss and sorrow began to subside?

A loved one had departed, whether it was a parent or even a dear friend, and you had been stricken with grief.

You missed them and dreaded the coming days of their absence...and then the sadness began to pass.

You still missed them.

You always would...but you took comfort in knowing they were now in a better place, and that they would always be with you as well.

They would never be forgotten.

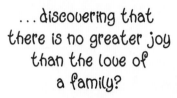

*...discovering that
there is no greater joy
than the love of
a family?*

You were loved and nurtured by your own mother,
    who taught you everything you needed to raise a
    family of your own.
What a gift it is, that capacity to love and be loved——a
    gift that is passed on to future generations.

...what motherhood is really all about?

A mother's lot is not an easy one.

She is blessed with a gift of a new life that she must
prize more than her own. All of her attention,
cares, concerns, and efforts will revolve around
this child.

It is the most important thing in her life.

All of the pain, the inconvenience, and the heartache
she endures willingly...her only reward is the
cherub's smile and the love of a child for its
mother.

This is the lot of a mother, and it will give her more
rewards than she ever dreamed of.

So many precious moments.

Where did all the time go?

First your mother was the most important person in your life.

Before you knew it, you were a mother yourself, raising a child of your own.

Now your child is nearly grown.

You still have your memories—memories you are able to share with your mother, your children, and even your grandchildren someday.

Angela Grace